CORNISH
FOR BEGINNERS

Angela Wilkes

Illustrated by John Shackell

Designed by Roger Priddy

Cornish Edition by Graham Sandercock

Technical Assistance: Stephen Beazley

CONTENTS

About this book

This book shows you that learning Cornish can be fun and prepares you for meeting other Cornish speakers in a variety of situations. Using the phrases from this book you will be able to talk about yourself and be involved in simple conversations.

You can find out how to . . .

talk about yourself,

and your home and family,

count and tell the time,

ask for the food you like,

find your way around,

and go shopping.

How you learn

The pictures show you what to say in each situation. Read the speech bubbles, and see how much you can understand by yourself. Then look up any words you do not know. Words and phrases are repeated again and again, to help you remember them. The book starts with things that are easy to say and gets harder as you go on.

New words

All the new words you come across are listed on each double page, so you can find them easily as you go along. If you forget a word, you can look it up in the vocabulary on pages 46-48. If you see an asterisk* by a word, it means there is a note about it at the bottom of the page.

Grammar

Cornish is easier if you know some of its grammar, or rules, but it doesn't matter if you don't understand it all straightaway. Boxes like this around words show where new grammar is explained. You can look up any of the grammar, including the rules about how Cornish word endings change, on pages 42-43.

How to say things

Cornish pronunciation is quite straightforward but a guide is given on page 41. On page 43 you can find out about Cornish words which change their first letters.

Puzzles

All the way through the book there are puzzles and quizzes to help you practise your Cornish and to test yourself on what you have learned. You can check whether your answers are right on pages 44-45.

Practising your Cornish

Write all the new words in a notebook, and try to learn a few every day. Keep going over them and you will soon remember them.

Ask a friend or someone in your family to test you. Better still, find someone to learn Cornish with you so you can practise on each other.

My a garsa ...

Try speaking Cornish whenever you can. Don't be afraid of making mistakes. No one will mind.

Saying hello and goodbye

The first thing you should know how to say in Cornish is 'Hello'. There are different greetings for different times of day. Here you can find out what to say when.

Try to learn the useful greetings in these pictures. The pronunciation guide on page 41 will help you to say the words properly

Saying 'Hello'

This is how to say 'Hello' to your friends.

This is how you say 'Good morning' to someone.

This is how you say 'Good evening' to someone.

Saying 'Goodbye'

Dyw genes means 'Goodbye'

Dha weles means 'see you!'

Saying 'Goodnight'

You only use **nos dha** last thing at night.

How are you?

This means 'How are you?'.

This woman is saying that she is alright, thank you....

...but this man is saying that he is in a bad way.

Fatla genes?

This list shows you different ways of saying how you are. What do you think these people would say if you asked them how they were?

pur dha	very well
yn poynt da	in good health
meur ras	thank you
da lowr	alright
yn studh drog	in a bad way
yn studh euthek	terrible

5

What is your name ?

Here you can find out how to ask someone their name and tell them yours, and how to introduce your friends. Read the picture strip and see how much you can understand. Then try doing the puzzles on the page opposite.

New words

pyth yw dha hanow?	what is your name?
ow hanow yw Jenifer	my name is Jenifer
Jenifer ov vy	Jenifer am I
ow hanow	my name
ow hanow yw	my name is
dha hanow	your name
y/hy hanow	his/her name
aga henwyn	their names
ev yw ow howeth	he is my friend
ow howethes	my (girl) friend
piw?	who?
piw yw ev?	who is he?
piw yw hi	who is she?
fatla genes?	how are you ?
yn poynt da	in good health
meur ras	thank you
yw!	yes it is!
nag yw!	no it's not!
mes	but

My, her, their

The Cornish words **ow**, **hy** and **aga** can change the first letter of the next word, for example **koweth**, friend, **ow howeth**, 'my friend'. These are explained on page 42. The words for 'your', **dha** and 'his', **y** cause a slightly different change, for example **dha goweth**, 'your friend'.

Introducing friends

What are they called?

Can you answer these questions in Cornish?

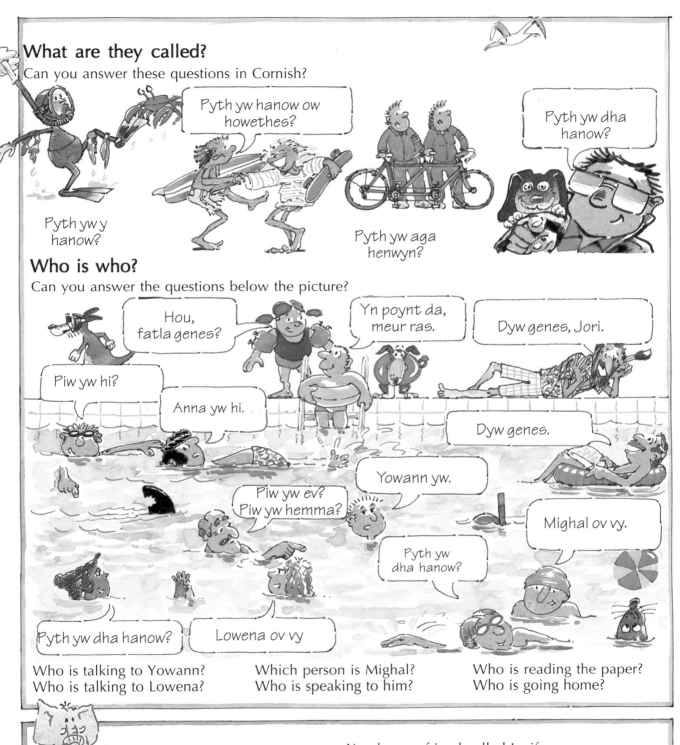

Pyth yw hanow ow howethes?

Pyth yw dha hanow?

Pyth yw y hanow?

Pyth yw aga henwyn?

Who is who?

Can you answer the questions below the picture?

Hou, fatla genes?

Yn poynt da, meur ras.

Dyw genes, Jori.

Piw yw hi?

Anna yw hi.

Dyw genes.

Yowann yw.

Piw yw ev?
Piw yw hemma?

Mighal ov vy.

Pyth yw dha hanow?

Pyth yw dha hanow?

Lowena ov vy

Who is talking to Yowann?
Who is talking to Lowena?

Which person is Mighal?
Who is speaking to him?

Who is reading the paper?
Who is going home?

Can you remember?

How would you ask someone's name?
How would you tell them your name?

You have a friend called Jenifer.
How would you introduce her?
How would you tell someone that your
friend's name is Gawen?

Finding out what things are called

Everything on this picture has its name on it. See if you can learn the names for everything, then try the memory test at the bottom of the next page.

You can find out how to say 'the' in Cornish at the bottom of this page.

chymbla

edhen

to

howl

Dydh da!

neyth

gwydhenn

fenester

bleujennow

daras

chi

karrji

Ottomma agan chi

ke

kath

ki

karr

Nouns

All Cornish nouns are masculine or feminine, indicated in the Glossary (pages 46-48) by the abbreviations m. and f.

The Cornish for 'the' is **an.** This can change the first letter of feminine nouns starting with certain letters. This is explained more fully on page 42.

an howl	the sun
an wydhenn	the tree (**gwydhenn**)
an to	the roof
an gath	the cat (**kath**)
an ki	the dog
an neyth	the nest

an edhen	the bird
an karrji	the garage
an chi	the house
an fenester	the window
an daras	the door
an bleujennow	the flowers (plural)

Asking what things are called

Don't worry if you don't know what something is called in Cornish. Just ask **pyth yw hemma/henna** (what is this/that?) Look at the list of useful phrases below, then read the picture strip to see how to use them

pyth yw hemma?	what is this?
pyth yw henna?	what is that?
yw henna ki?	is that a dog?
nag yw	no it's not
ynwedh	also
yn Kernewek	in Cornish
yn Sowsnek	in English
ha	and

Can you remember?
Cover up the word lists, and see if you can name these things in Cornish. Start with the thing you are naming: **ki yw** (a dog it is)

There is no word in Cornish for 'a' or 'an', so to say 'a flower' you use the noun on its own: **bleujenn**.

9

Where do you come from?

Here you can find out how to ask people where they come from. You can also find out if they can speak Cornish

New Words

a bleth os ta devedhys?	where do you come from?
devedhys ov a	I come from
pleth os ta trigys?	where do you live?
	I live in
trigys ov yn	I speak
my a gews	do you speak?
a wre'ta kewsel?	a little
nebes	Cornish
Kernewek	English
Sowsnek	French
Frynkek	Welsh
Kembrek	Spanish
Spaynek	yes I do
gwrav	

Countries

Almayn	Germany
Pow Frynk	France
Pow Sows	England
Kembra	Wales
Alban	Scotland
Spayn	Spain
Russi	Russia
Eynda	India
Iwerdhon	Ireland
Kernow	Cornwall

Where do you come from?

A ble'th os ta devedhys?

Devedhys ov a Gernow.

Ple'th os ta trigys?

Trigys ov yn Pennsans.

A ble'th os ta devedhys?

Devedhys ov a Almayn.

Devedhys yw ow howethes a Bow Frynk. Trigys yw hi yn Paris

Can you speak Cornish?

A wre'ta kewsel Kernewek?

Gwrav, nebes.

A wre'ta kewsel Frynkek, Jenifer?

Gwrav, my a gews Frynkek ha nebes Spaynek.

Henri a gews Kernewek, Sowsnek ha Kembrek.

10   **a,** 'from' can change the first letter of the next word, **Kernow,** 'Cornwall' but **a Gernow,** 'from Cornwall'

Who comes from where?

These are the contestants for an international dancing competition. They have come from all over the world. The compère cannot speak any Cornish and does not understand where anyone comes from. Read about the contestants, then see if you can tell him what he wants to know. His questions are beneath the picture.

Devedhys yw Angus a Alban.

Ottomma Marie ha Pierre. Devedhys yns a Bow Frynk.

Hari hag Indira yw devedhys a Eynda.

Devedhys yw Yuri a Russi. Trigys yw ev yn Moskow.

Devedhys yw Hans a Almayn.

Ottomma Lolita! Devedhys yw hi a Spayn.

A ble'th yns i oll devedhys?

Who lives in Moscow?
Is there a Scottish contestant?
Where do Marie and Pierre come from?

Where does Hans come from?
What are the names of the Indians?
Is Lolita Italian or Spanish?

Verbs (action words)

Cornish has two forms of the verb 'to be'. The short form is used with nouns and adjectives; the long form is used with position and the present participle.

bos	to be (short form)	bos	to be (long form)
ov vy	am I	esov vy	am I
os ta	are you	esos ta	are you
yw ev/hi	is he/she	yma ev/hi	is he/she
on ni	are we	eson ni	are we
owgh hwi	are you	esowgh hwi	are you
yns i	are they	ymons i	are they

Can you remember?

How would you ask someone where they come from?
How do you say that you can speak Cornish?

Can you say where you come from?
How do you ask someone else if they can speak Cornish?

11

More about you

Here you can find out how to say how old you are, how many brothers and sisters you have, and how to count up to 10.

To say 'I have' in Cornish you say **yma dhymm** = 'there is to me' or **yma genev** = 'there is with me'

New words

pes?	how many?
pes bloedh?	how many years?
eus?	is/are there?
dhis	to you
yma dhymm	I have (own)
po	or
broder	brother
hwoer	sister
nyns eus dhymm	I don't have
ogas ha	nearly
yma genev	I have (with me)

yma dhymm means literally 'there is to me' so **yma ki dhymm** means 'I have or own a dog'.

yma genev means literally 'there is with me' so **yma ki genev** means 'I have a dog' but it may not be mine On the next page both forms are shown

Numbers*

1 onan
2 dew, diw
3 tri, teyr
4 peswar, peder
5 pymp
6 hwegh
7 seyth
8 eth
9 naw
10 deg

How old are you?

Pes bloedh os ta?

Deg bloedh ov vy, ha ty?

Unnek bloedh ov vy.

Have you any brothers or sisters?

Eus broder po hwoer dhis?

Eus, yma broder ha hwoer dhymm.

Pes bloedh yns i?

Peder yw seyth bloedh ha Maria yw hwegh bloedh.

Nyns eus na broder na hwoer dhymm.

*There is a longer list of numbers on page 40

How old are they ?

Read what these children are saying, then see if you can say how old they are.

Jori yw dewdhek bloedh.

Ni yw pymthek bloedh.

Morwenna yw unnek bloedh.

Mighal yw ogas ha peswardhek bloedh.

My yw pymp bloedh. Ev yw naw bloedh

Mighal   Maria ha Kerys   Jori   Morwenna   Dewi   Talwynn

How many brothers and sisters?

Below you can read how many brothers and sisters the children have. Can you work out who has which brothers and sisters?

Yma dhe Varia ha Kerys unn broder ha diw hwoer

Yma dhe Vorwenna teyr hwoer ha dew vroder

Yma dhe Vighal pymp hwoer mes nyns eus broder dhodho

Yma dhe Dhewi unn broder mes nyns eus hwoer dhodho

Nyns eus na broder na hwoer dhe Jori mes yma ki dhodho

'To have'

yma	dhymm/genev	I have
yma	dhis/genes	you have (s)
yma	dhodho/ganso	he has
yma	dhedhi/gensi	she has
yma	dhyn/genen	we have
yma	dhywgh/genowgh	you have (pl)
yma	dhedha/gansa	they have

nyns eus	dhymm/genev	I haven' t
nyns eus	dhis/genes	you haven't
nyns eus	dhodho/ganso	he hasn't
nyns eus	dhedhi/gensi	she hasn't
nyns eus	dhyn/genen	we haven't
nyns eus	dhywgh/genowgh	you haven't
nyns eus	dhedha/gansa	they haven't

dhe 'to' causes a change to some letters; see page 42

Talking about your family

You will find lots of words on these two pages to help you talk about your family. Many of the phrases include the words 'my' and 'your', which you first learned on page 6.

Ottomma ow theylu.

ow hi

ow thas-gwynn

ow thas

ow hwoer

ow ewnter

ow hath

ow mamm-wynn

ow mamm

ow broder

ow modrep

Who's who?

Yw hemma dha vroder?

Yw, hemm yw ow broder.

Yw homma dha hwoer?

Yw. Hy hanow yw Lowena.

Yw an re ma dha gerens?

Na! Ow herens-wynn yns i.

New words

teylu	family	**my yw**	I am	**tanow**	thin
kerens	parents	**ewnter**	uncle	**gols**	hair
tas	father	**modrep**	aunt	**melyn**	blonde, yellow
mamm	mother	**hir**	tall, long	**gell**	brown
tas-gwynn	grandfather	**bras**	big, large	**hegar**	affectionate
mamm-wynn	grandmother	**byghan**	small	**koth**	old
		tew	fat	**yns i**	are they

'My' and 'your'

The words for 'my' **ow** and 'your' **dha** can change (mutate) the first letter of the next word, as shown on the right: **ow** changes **k, p, t**; **dha** changes **b, d, g, k, m, p** and **t**.

ki > ow hi
penn > ow fenn
tas > ow thas

broder> dha vroder
dydh > dha dhydh
gols > dha wols
gweli > dha weli

ki > dha gi
mamm > dha vamm
penn > dha benn
tas > dha das

hemma, hemm (m.); **homma, homm** (f.) this; **an re ma**, these ones

Describing your family

Ow thas yw bras hag ow mamm yw byghan.

Ow mamm yw hir hag ow thas yw byghan.

Ow ewnter yw tew hag ow modryp yw tanow.

Ow thas-gwynn yw koth mes my yw yowynk.

Yma gols melyn dhe'm hwoer ha gols gell dhe'm broder.

Ow hi yw hegar.

Describing words

In Cornish you do not say 'a big dog' but 'dog big': **ki bras**. Like some nouns, adjectives (describing words) can change or mutate softly: **byghan** 'small' but 'a small cat', **kath vyghan**.

Can you describe each of these people in Cornish, using the new words you have learned. Start with the adjective followed by ... **yw ev.**

Your home

Here you can find out how to say what sort of home you live in, and where it is. You can also learn what all the rooms are called.

New words

po	or
chi	house
rannji	flat
kastell	castle
y'n dre	in the town
y'n pow	in the country
ryb an mor	by the sea
tas	Dad
mamm	Mum
tarosvann	ghost
ple'th esos ta?	where are you?
stevell-omwolghi	bathroom
stevell-dhybri	dining-room
chambour	bedroom
esedhva	living room
kegin	kitchen
hel	hall
leur	storey
war-wartha	upstairs
tas-gwynn	grandfather
mamm-wynn	grandmother
trigys ov vy yn	I live in
piw eus?	who is? (place)
ple'ma?	where is/are?

Where do you live?

Ple'th os ta trigys?

Trigys ov vy yn chi.

Trigys ov vy yn rannji.

Trigys ov vy yn kastell.

Town or country?

Trigys ov vy y'n dre.

Trigys ov vy y'n pow.

Trigys ov vy ryb an mor.

16

Where is everyone?

Dad comes home and wants to find out where everyone is. Look at the pictures and see if you can tell him. (For example, **yma mamm y'n** chambour) Then see if you can answer the questions below the little pictures.

mamm   tas   tas-gwynn

mamm-wynn   Peder   Isabella

Simon   an tarosvann

Piw eus y'n stevell-dhybri?
Piw eus y'n gegin?
Piw eus y'n stevell-omwolghi?
Piw eus y'n chambour?

Ple'ma mamm-wynn?
Ple'ma an tarosvann?
Ple'ma Isabella?
Ple'ma Peder?
Ple'ma tas?

Yth esov vy y'n stevell-omwolghi.

Yth esov vy war-wartha.

Yth esov vy yn chambour Isabella

Yth esov vy y'n esedhva.

Yth esov vy y'n chambour.

Ple'th esos ta?

Yth esov vy y'n stevell-dhybri.

Yth esov vy y'n gegin.

Can you remember?

Cover up the pictures and see if you can remember how to say these things. The answers are on page 44.

I live in a town.
You live in the country.
Grandma lives in a flat.

We live in a house.
The bedroom is upstairs.
Simon is in the bath.

yth esov vy = 'I am', long form of 'to be'

17

Looking for things

Here you can find out how to ask someone what they are looking for and tell them where things are. You can also learn lots of words for things around the house.

New words

ow hwiles	looking for
ow kul	doing
neppyth	something
hamster	a hamster
kavoes	to find
y	him
y'n amari	in the cupboard
yn-dann	under
a-dryv	behind
yn mysk	among
gweli-dydh	sofa
kador	chair
kroglenn	curtain
bleujennow	flowers
moes	table
estyllenn	shelf
leurlenn	carpet
pellwolok	television
pellgowser	telephone
seth	vase

Yma, usi, eus

These are all used when you are saying where something is or what somebody is doing.

yma means 'there is', there are' or sometimes 'is'

usi is used instead of **yma** when asking question; so **usi ev** means 'is he?'

eus means 'is there?', or 'are there?'

The missing hamster

Pyth esos ta ow kul?

Yth esov vy ow hwiles ow hamster. Ny allav vy y gavoes

Nyns usi ev war an amari.

Nyns usi ev yn-dann an gweli-dydh.

Usi ev a-dryv an groglenn?

Nag usi!

Ottomma! Yn mysk an bleujennow.

In, on or under?

y'n gyst means 'in the box'. To say where something is use **yma**; so **yma an hamster y'n gyst** means 'the hamster is in the box'.

Each of the words below can be followed by **an** 'the'.

yn

a-dryv

a-rag

ryb   yn-dann   war

Where are the animals hiding?

Grandfather's six pets are hiding somewhere in the room but he cannot find them. Can you tell him where they are in Cornish, using the words above?

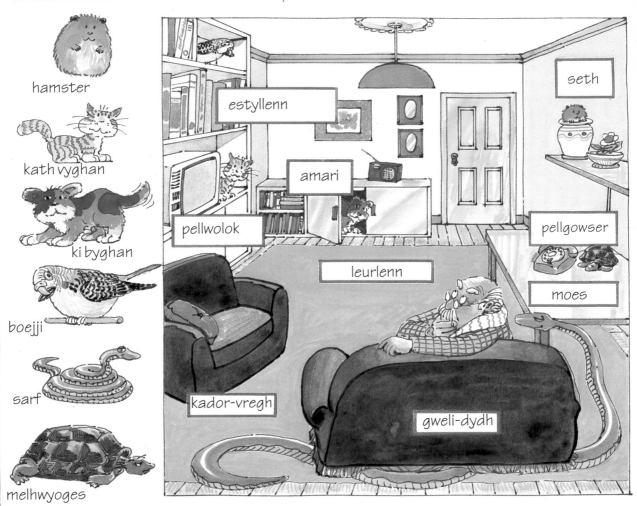

hamster

kath vyghan

ki byghan

boejji

sarf

melhwyoges

estyllenn

amari

pellwolok

leurlenn

kador-vregh

gweli-dydh

seth

pellgowser

moes

What do you like eating?

Here you can learn lots of food words and find out how to say what you like and don't like.

New Words

yw da genes?	do you like?
da yw genev	I like
nyns yw da genev	I don't like
dybri	to eat
ow tybri	eating
pyth?	what?
ytho?	then?
tamm vydh	not at all
gwell	better
gwell yw genev	I prefer
an gwella oll	the best of all
letus	lettuce
pysk	fish
askloes	chips
tesenn	cake
selsik	sausages
kig	meat
spagetti	spaghetti
pitsa	pizza
hamburger	hamburger
ris	rice
bara	bread
keus	cheese
my ynwedh	me too

What would you like?

Yw da genes dybri letus?

Nag yw, nyns yw da genev dybri letus.

Yw da genes dybri pysk?

Nag yw, tamm vydh!

Pyth yw da genes ytho?

Da yw genev dybri askloes.

An gwella oll genev yw tesenn.

What do you like most ?

Pyth yw gwell genes?

Da yw genev dybri selsik.

Mes gwell yw genev dybri kig.

Ha'n gwella oll genev yw spagetti.

What are they eating?

Pyth esos ta ow tybri?

Yth esov vy ow tybri pitsa.

Yma hi ow tybri askloes.

Yma ev ow tybri bara gans keus.

Yth eson ni ow tybri hamburgers.

Yth esowgh hwi ow tybri ris.

Ymons i ow tybri bananas.

Who likes what ?

Who likes cheese ? Who likes ham?
Who prefers grapes to bananas?

Can you say in Cornish which things you like and which you don't like?

My ynwedh mes nyns yw, da genev mordhos hogh.

Da yw genev dybri bananas.

Gwell yw genev dybri gwinreun.

Da yw genev dybri keus.

Gwell yw genev dybri hogen froeth.

Yowann

Davydh

Tas-gwynn

Pyran

Beth

mordhos hogh

amanenn

pitsa

bara

salad

avalow kerensa

keus

bananas

gwinreun

hogenn froeth

sugen froeth

bos 'to be' (long form*)

yth esov vy	I am	nyns esov vy	I 'm not	yth eson ni	we are	nyns eson ni	we aren't
yth esos ta	you are	nyns esos ta	you aren't	yth esowgh hwi	you are	nyns esowgh hwi	you aren't
yma ev/hi	he/she is	nyns usi ev/hi	he/she isn't	yth esons i	they are	nyns esons i	they aren't

* used with position/place and actions

21

Table talk

Here you can learn about things to say during a meal.

New Words

dywgh!	come (plural)!
dhe'n voes!	to the table!
moes	table
boes	food
mar pleg	please
meur ras	thanks
yma nown dhymm	I am hungry
eus nown dhis?	are you hungry?
pur dha	very good
ystynn dhymm	pass me
dowr	water
bara	bread
gwedrenn	a glass
kig	meat
omserv!	help yourself!
hwans	wish
eus hwans dhis?	do you want
eus	yes (there is)
nag eus	no (there isn't)
my re dhybris	I have eaten enough
lowr	
yw an boes da?	is the food good?
yw	yes (it is)
pur dha yw	it's very good

Dinner is ready

Dywgh dhe'n voes, mar pleg!

Yma nown dhymm.

Dhymm ynwedh.

Omserv, mar pleg!

Meur ras.

Eus nown dhis?

Eus; an boes yw pur dha!

Please will you pass me...

Ystynn dhymm an dowr, mar pleg.

Ystynn dhymm an bara, mar pleg.

Ystynn dhymm gwedrenn, mar pleg.

Would you like some more?

Who is saying what ?

These little pictures show different mealtime situations. Cover up the rest of the page and see if you know what each of them would say in Cornish.

Jori is saying that he is hungry.

The chef wants you to enjoy your meal.

Jenefer is saying 'Help yourself'.

Peder wants someone to give him a glass.

Jori's mother asks him if he wants any chips.

He says 'Yes, please. I like chips.'

Then he says 'No thanks, I've eaten enough.'

Mark is saying the food tastes delicious.

You

As in many languages, there are two words for 'you' in Cornish: **ty** is the singular form used when addressing one person and **hwi** is the plural when you are talking to more than one person.

23

Your hobbies

These people are talking about their hobbies.

New words

lymna	to paint
kegi	to cook
da yw genev	I like to
gwruthyl traow	to make things
donsya	to dance
redya	to read
mires orth	to look at
gwia	to weave/knit
neuvya	to swim
goslowes orth	to listen to
sport	sport
seni	to play (music)
gwari	to play (game)
peldroes	football
tennis	tennis
ilow	music
daffar	musical
ilow	instrument
krowd	violin
piano	piano
y'n gorthugher	in the evening
dell yw usyes	usually
lyvrow	books
hobi	hobby

Verbs

In Cornish you can say 'I swim' **my a* neuv** or 'I am swimming' **yth esov vy ow* neuvya.**

my a sen	I play
ev a sen	he plays
hi a red	she reads
yth esov ow redya	I am reading
yma hi ow redya	she is reading
a wre'ta?	do you (s.)
a wre'ta gwari?	do you play?
a wrewgh hwi?	do you (p.)

Pyth yw da genes y wul?

Da yw genev lymna ...

... mes nyns yw da genev kegi.

Pyth yw dha hobi?

Da yw genev gwruthyl traow ...

... ha da yw genev donsya.

What do you do in the evenings?

Pandr'a wre'ta y'n gorthuger?

My a red lyvrow...

... po mires orth an bellwolok po gwia.

a and **ow** can cause changes to the next word

24

The sporty type

Pyth yw dha hobi?

Da yw genev sport.

My a neuv.

My a wari peldroes.

My a wari tennis.

Music lovers

Pyth yw da genowgh?

Da yw genen goslowes orth ilow.

A wrewgh hwi seni daffar ilow?

My a sen an piano.

My a sen an krowd.

What are they doing?

A

B

C

D

E

Cover up the rest of the page and see if you can say in Cornish what all these people are doing, e.g. **yma ev ow ...** or **yma hi ow ...** Can you say in Cornish what your hobbies are?

25

Telling the time

Here you can find out how to tell and ask the time in Cornish.

You can look up numbers on page 40: **eur** 'hour', 'o'clock' is feminine, so 2, 3 and 4 use the feminine forms, **diw, teyr, peder. dhe** 'to' can change the next word (see page 42). There are more numbers on page 40.

What is the time?

This is how you ask the time.

New words

py eur yw?	what is the time?
unn eur	one o'clock
diw eur	two o'clock
pymp mynysenn dhe/wosa	five minutes to/past
kwarter dhe/ wosa	a quarter to/ past
hanter wosa deg	half past ten
hanterdydh	midday, noon
hanternos	midnight
myttin	morning
myttinweyth	in the morning
gorthugher	evening
gorthugherweyth	in the evening
sevel	to rise, get up
skol	school
mos dhe'n skol	go to school
gweli	bed
mos dhe'n gweli	to go to bed

The time is...

Pymp mynysenn wosa naw yw.

Kwarter wosa naw yw.

Hanter wosa naw yw.

Kwarter dhe dheg yw.

Pymp mynysenn dhe dheg yw.

Hanternos/ hanterdydh yw.

What time of day?

Mealtimes

prys-boes	mealtime
hansel	breakfast
li	lunch
kinyow	dinner
te	tea
soper	supper

Hwegh eur myttinweyth yw.

Hwegh eur gorthugherweyth yw.

Mark's day

Read what Mark does during the day, then see if you can match each clock with the right picture. You can check your answers on page 44-45.

 a
 b
 c
 d
 e
 f
 g
 h

1 Yma Mark ow sevel dhe hanter wosa hwegh.

2 Yma ev ow tybri hansel dhe eth eur.

3 Yma ev ow mos dhe'n skol dhe gwarter dhe naw.

4 Yma ev ow tybri liv dhe hanter wosa hanterdydh.

5 Yma ev ow kwari peldroes dhe dhiw eur.

6 Yma ev ow mires orth an bellwolok dhe bymp eur

7 Yma ev ow tybri kinyow dhe hwegh eur.

8 Yma ev ow mos dhe'n gweli dhe hanter wosa eth.

What is the time?

Can you say in Cornish what times these clocks show?

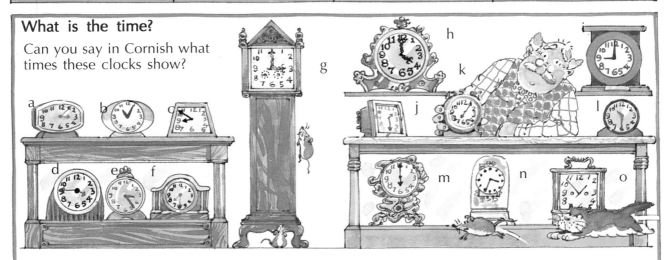

note the changes of some letters after **ow** '-ing' (see page 42)

27

Arranging things

Here is how to arrange to do things with your friends.

New words

a vynn'ta?	do you want to?
p'eur?	when?
bys yn	until
dos	to come
mos	to go
pur dha	very well
hedhyw	today
dohajydh	afternoon
dohajydhweyth	in the afternoon
a-vorow	tomorrow
war tu ha	towards, about
ny allav	I can't
dha weles!	see you!
haneth	tonight
poll neuvya	swimming pool
da lowr	OK, fair enough
kevywi	party
dons	dance
ytho	then, so
gav dhymm	excuse me

Days of the week

dy' Lun	Monday
dy' Meurth	Tuesday
dy' Mergher	Wednesday
dy' Yow	Thursday
dy' Gwener	Friday
dy' Sadorn	Saturday
dy' Sul	Sunday

Tennis

Swimming

Going to the cinema

Going to a party

Your diary for the week

This is your diary for the week. Read it and see if you can answer the questions.

What are you doing on Friday evening ?
When are you playing tennis ?
What are you doing on Tuesday afternoon?

dy' Lun
4 eur: tennis

dy' Meurth
2 eur: piano
5.30 eur: poll neuvya

dy' Mergher
3 eur: tennis
7.45 eur: sinema

dy' Yow

dy' Gwener
8. eur donsya gans Jori

dy' Sadorn
2 eur: peldroes
7 eur: kyvewi

dy' Sul
dohajydh:
tennis

What are you doing?

Pandr'a wre'ta dy'Gwener?
Dy' Gwener, my a wra donsya.

What are you doing on Friday?
On Friday, I will be dancing.

my a wra = 'I do', 'I will'

Asking the way

The next three pages show you how to find your way around.

New Words

gav dhymm	excuse me
yn hons	over there
a dravydh	it's no trouble
ple'ma an ...?	where is the ...?
Soedhva an Post	Post Office
gorsav	station
ryb	by, next to
a-dal	opposite
stret	street
eglos	church
gwesti	guest house
marghas	market
yn ogas	nearby
treyl a-gledh!	turn left!
yw pell?	is it far?
hag ena	and then
mynysenn	a minute
war droes	on foot
koffiji	coffee house
kymyst	chemist
arghantti	bank
a-dal	opposite
gorvarghas	supermarket

Being polite

Gav dhymm ...

Meur ras dhis.

A dravydh!

Where is ...?

Ple'ma Soedhva an Post, mar pleg?

Yn hons, ryb an varghas.

Ple'ma Gwesti an Gorsav, mar pleg?

Treyl a-gledh hag ena war ewn.

Directions

war ewn

a-gledh   a-dheghow

Is there a . . . nearby?

Is it far?

Other useful places to ask for

gorsav	gorsav betrol	privedhyow	kyst lytherow
railway station	garage	toilets	postbox
log pellgowser	kampva	klavji	ayrborth
telephone box	camp site	hospital	airport

Finding your way around

Here you can find out how to ask your way around and follow directions. When you have read everything else, try the map puzzle on the opposite page.

New words

treylya	to turn	soedhva dherivadow	tourist office
kemmeres	to take	hel an dre	town hall
lywya	to drive	gwerthji	shop
y'n karr	by car	boesti	restaurant
kynsa stret	first street	ostel	hotel
eyl stret	next street	eglos	church
ostel yowynkneth	youth hostel	ena	then, there

Giving directions

The imperative is the part of the verb you use for giving orders. In Cornish you usually drop the verb ending: **treylya** 'to turn', **treyl**; 'turn!'; **kemmeres** 'to take', **kemmer** 'take!'; **lywya** 'to drive', **lyw** 'drive!'. Some common verbs are irregular: **mos** 'to go', **ke;** 'go'; **dos** 'to come', **deus;** 'come!'

Finding your way around Trenowydh

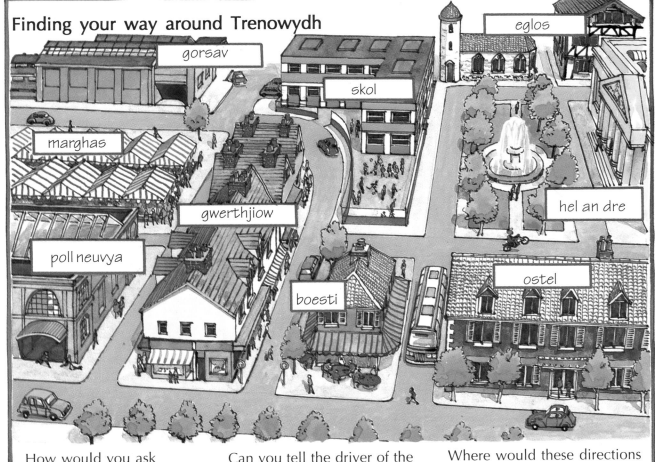

gorsav · skol · eglos · marghas · gwerthjiow · hel an dre · poll neuvya · boesti · ostel

How would you ask someone the way to the market place? How would you ask if there is a café nearby?

Can you tell the driver of the red car how to get to the station? Then tell the driver of the yellow car how to get to the church.

Where would these directions take the yellow car?
Kemmer an eyl stret a-gledh hag ena a-dheghow.

Going shopping

Here you can find out what to say in Cornish when you go shopping.

New words

prena	to buy
hi a bren	she buys
prenassa	to go shopping
boes	food
popti	bakery
spisti	grocer's
kikti	butcher's
leth	milk
oy	egg
froeth	fruit
losow-kegin	vegetables
kig	meat
bara byghan	roll, bun
aval	apple
aval-kerensa	tomato
yw henna oll?	is that all?
pandr'a vynn'ta?	what do you want?
arghans	money
neppyth arall?	anything else?
py kost yw?	how much is it?
oll warbarth	all together
liter	litre
kilo	kilo

Mrs Gwynn goes shopping

Yma Mestres Gwynn ow prenassa.

POPTI

Y'n popti, hi a bren bara.

In the baker's

Dydh da!

Dydh da, Mestres Gwynn!

Peswar bara byghan, mar pleg.

Yw henna oll?

Unn peuns, mar pleg.

Yw, meur ras. Py kost yw?

Ottomma! Meur ras!

£1

Plurals

The most common way to make a plural noun in Cornish is to add -ow to the singular: **chi**, 'house', **chiow**, 'houses'.
However there are many exceptions and these are shown in the Glossary on pages 46-48, so **edhen f. ydhyn** *bird* means that **edhen** is 'a bird' and **ydhyn** means 'birds'.

Y'n spisti, hi a bren leth hag oyow.

Y'n varghas, hi a bren froeth ha losow-kegin.

Y'n kikti, hi a bren kig.

At the grocer's

Pandr'a vynn'ta?

Hwegh oy, mar pleg.

Neppyth arall?

Liter a leth, mar pleg.

Py kost yw henna?

Henn yw unn peuns ha tri-ugens diner.

£1.60

At the market

Dydh da! Pandr'a vynn'ta?

Kilo a avalow, mar pleg.

Neppyth arall?

Kilo a avalow-kerensa.

Henn yw dew beuns ha peswar-ugens diner.

£2.80

*You will find a list of Cornish numbers on page 40.

Shopping and going to a café

Here you can find out how to ask how much things cost and how to order in a café.

New words

gwinreun	grapes
kartenn bost	postcard
rosenn	rose
reken	bill
owraval	orange
sugen	juice
pinaval	pineapple
lymmaval	lemon
lymmaval	lemonade
brykedh	apricots
kola	cola
te	tea
gans leth	with milk
choklet	chocolate
poeth	hot
dyenn rew	ice-cream
my a garsa	I would like
gwedrennas	a glass
koffi	a café, coffee
py kost yw ?	how much does...cost?
kemmeres	to take
my a gemmer	I'll take

Asking how much things cost

Py kost yw an gartenn bost ma?

Dew-ugens diner.

Py kost yw an gwinreun?

Dew beuns an kilo.

£2.00

Py kost yw an rosennow?

Unn peuns pub huni.

£1.00

My a gemmer seyth, mar pleg.

Going to a café

Pandr'a vynn'ta?

Koffi, mar pleg!

Ottomma!

Meur ras.

An reken, mar pleg.

Henn yw peuns hag ugens.

36

Buying fruit

Everything on the fruit stall is marked with its name and price. Look at the picture, then see if you can answer the questions below it.

AVALOW
an kilo
£2.00

Pandr'a vynn'ta?

BANANAS
an kilo
£1.80

GWINREUN
an kilo
£2.10

OWRAVALOW
an kilo
£1.80

PINAVALOW
pub huni
£1.60

BRYKEDH
an kilo
£1.80

LYMMAVALOW
pub huni
£0.20

How do you tell the stallholder you would like four lemons, a kilo of bananas and a pineapple? How much do each of these things cost? How much is the total?

Py kost yw avalow an kilo?
Py kost yw unn pinaval?
Py kost yw brykedh an kilo?
Py kost yw bananas an kilo?

In the café

Here are some things you might order in a café.

My a garsa ...

lymmaval	kola
te gans leth	te gans lymmaval
sugen	choklet poeth
gwedrennas leth	dyenn rew

Months, seasons and dates

Here you can learn what the seasons and months are called and find out how to say what the date is.

New Words

blydhen	year
mis	month
penn-bloedh	birthday
hedhyw	today
py dydh?	what day?
an jydh	the day date

The seasons

gwenton	spring
hav	summer
kynyav	autumn
gwav	winter

The months

mis-Genver	January
mis-Hwevrer	February
mis-Meurth	March
mis-Ebryl	April
mis-Me	May
mis-Metheven	June
mis-Gortheren	July
mis-Est	August
mis-Gwynngala	September
mis-Hedra	October
mis-Du	November
mis-Kevardhu	December

The seasons

Gwenton

Meurth, Ebryl, Me

Hav

Metheven, Gortheren, Est

Kynyav

Gwynngala, Hedra, Du

Gwav

Kevardhu, Genver, Hwevrer

First, second, third

kynsa (!a)	first
nessa (2a)	second
tressa (3a)	third
peswara (4a)	fourth
pympes (5es)	fifth
hweghves (6ves)	sixth
seythves (7ves)	seventh
ethves (8ves)	eighth
nawves (9ves)	ninth
degves (10ves)	tenth
ugensves (20ves)	twentieth
degves warn ugens (30ens)	thirtieth

> Mis-Genver yw kynsa mis an vlydhen.

> Mis-Hwevrer yw nessa mis an vlydhen.

> Mis-Hedra yw degves mis an vlydhen.

Can you say where the rest of the months come in the year?

-ens is the abbreviation for numbers after 21

What is the date*?

Hedhyw yw an tressa a vis Me.

Py dydh yw hedhyw?

An kynsa a vis Genver.

Writing the date

Rysrudh an 3a a vis Me

Here you can see how a date is written; 'of' is expressed by **a** which changes **mis** to **vis**.

When is your birthday?

Py dydh yw dha benn-bloedh?

An degves a vis Du.

Ow fenn-bloedh yw an dewdhegves a vis Hwevrer.

Penn-bloedh Simon yw an ethves a vis Metheven.

When are their birthdays?

The dates of the children's birthdays are written below their pictures. Can you say in Cornish when they are (e.g. **penn-bloedh Morwenna yw an nessa a vis Ebryl**)?

Morwenna	Wella	Tegenn	Maria	Alan	Dewi

an 2a a vis Ebryl	an 21ens a vis Metheven	an 18ves a vis Hedra	an 31ens a vis Est	an 3a a vis Meurth	an 7ves a vis Gwynngala

* **dydh**, 'a day', **an jydh** 'the day'

Colours and numbers

Colours are adjectives (describing words), so in Cornish they come after the word they refer to, e.g. **gols du** (black hair), **ki gwynn** (white dog).

The colours

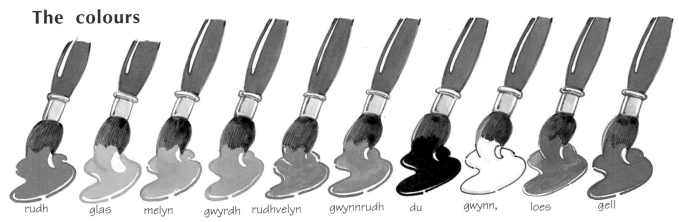

rudh   glas   melyn   gwyrdh   rudhvelyn   gwynnrudh   du   gwynn,   loes   gell

What colour is it?

Cover up the picture above and see if can you say what colour everything is in the painting. (You can check the answers on page 45.)

Numbers

*Cornish counts in twenties; from 21 to 39 you use **warn ugens**; from 41 to 59 you use **ha dew-ugens;** from 61 to 79 **ha tri-ugens** and so on. So 36 is **hwetek warn ugens**; 59 **nownsek ha dew-ugens** etc.

1	onan	11	unnek	21	onan warn ugens	31	unnek warn ugens
2	dew	12	dewdhek	22	dew warn ugens	40	dew-ugens
3	tri	13	trydhek	23	tri warn ugens	50	deg ha dew-ugens
4	peswar	14	peswardhek	24	peswar warn ugens	60	tri-ugens
5	pymp	15	pymthek	25	pymp warn ugens	70	deg ha tri-ugens
6	hwegh	16	hwetek	26	hwegh warn ugens	80	peswar-ugens
7	seyth	17	seytek	27	seyth warn ugens	90	deg ha peswar ugens
8	eth	18	etek	28	eth warn ugens	100	kans
9	naw	19	nownsek	29	naw warn ugens	200	dew kans
10	deg	20	ugens	30	deg warn ugens	1000	mil

Pronunciation and grammar

Consonants

The following Cornish consonants are pronounced as in English:
b, d, f, h, j, k, l, m, n, p, s, t, v, w.
The Cornish **'dh'** is like English 'th' in words like 'the', 'this'.
The Cornish **'g'** is always like the 'g' in English 'game' (never like the 'g' in English 'gem').
The Cornish **'gh'** is pronounced at the end of a word like the 'ch' in Scottish 'loch'. In the middle of a word it is an 'h' sound.
The Cornish **'r'** is slightly rolled.
The Cornish **'th'** is like the English 'th' in 'thistle'.
Cornish **'ch'** and **'sh'** are pronounced as in English.
Cornish **'y'** as a consonant is pronunced like the 'y' in English 'yes'.

Vowels

a	like English b<u>a</u>t	e.g. **kath**, 'cat'
e	like English b<u>e</u>t	e.g. **penn**, 'head'
eu	like French b<u>eu</u>rre	e.g. **meur**, 'great'
i	like English b<u>ee</u>f	e.g. **mis**, 'month'
o	like English b<u>o</u>mb	e.g. **mos**, 'to go'
oe	like French b<u>eau</u>	e.g. **froeth**, 'fruit'
ou	like English b<u>oo</u>t	e.g. **gour**, 'husband'
u	like French b<u>u</u>	e.g. **gul**, 'to do'
y	like English b<u>i</u>n	e.g. **dydh**, 'day'

Dipthongs

ay	like English b<u>y</u>	e.g. **ayr**, 'air'
aw	like English b<u>ow</u> d<u>ow</u>n	e.g. **maw**, 'boy'
ew	like Welsh t<u>ew</u> (like 'e-oo' said quickly)	e.g. **rew**, 'ice'
ey	like English b<u>ai</u>l	e.g. **neyth**, 'nest'
iw/yw	like Welsh b<u>iw</u> (like 'i-oo' said quickly)	e.g. **piw**, 'who'
ow	like English b<u>ow</u> and arr<u>ow</u>	e.g. **nown**, 'hunger'
oy	like English b<u>oy</u>	e.g. **oy**, 'egg'

Vowel length

If a word ends in a double consonant, the vowel length is short e.g. **gell**, 'brown'; **penn**, 'head'

If a word ends in a single consonant, the vowel length is long e.g. **pel**, 'ball'; **deg**, 'ten'

Accentuation

Cornish words of more than one syllable are usually stressed on the next to last syllable:

dysk<u>a</u>dor, 'teacher'
but **dyskad<u>o</u>ryon**, 'teachers'

gw<u>e</u>li, 'bed'
but **gwel<u>i</u>ow**, 'beds'

Grammar

Grammar is like a set of rules about how you put words together and it is different for every language. You will find Cornish easier to learn if you learn some of its grammar but don't worry if you don't understand it all straightaway.

The verb 'to be' bos

There are two forms of the verb 'to be' in Cornish:

1. the short form, used with nouns and adjectives:

... ov vy	I am
... os ta	you are
... yw ev	he/it is
... yw hi	she/it is
... on ni	we are
... owgh hwi	you are
... yns i	they are

examples:
modrep yw hi   she is an aunt
skwith ov vy   I am tired

2. the long form, used with position and action (**ow⁴**):

yth esov vy	I am
yth esos ta	you are
yma ev	he/it is
yma hi	she/it is
yth eson ni	we are
yth esowgh hwi	you are
ymons i	they are

examples:
yma ev y'n gegin   he is in the kitchen
yth eson ni ow tybri   we are eating

To make any of these negative, you start with **nyns**:

nyns ov vy skwith   I am not tired
nyns eson ni ow tybri   we are not eating

but note that **yma** changes to **nyns usi**:

nyns usi hi ow tos   she is not coming

Table of mutations

Mutations are the changes to the first letter of a word. Column 1 in the table at the top of page 43 shows the letters which can mutate and columns 2, 3, 4, and 5 what they can change into.

Don't worry if you forget to make the changes but just knowing that they can happen helps to spot words which have changed. The most important changes which you find in this book are shown in the table below.

The soft or second mutation (column 2) is most common, occurring after **an** with feminine nouns beginning with the letters in column 1 and adjectives which follow them:

kath cat   **an gath**   the cat
gwynn white   **an gath wynn** the white cat

It also occurs after the words **dhe**, 'to' or 'at'; **dha** 'your', **y** 'his':

pymp eur   5 o'clock
dhe bymp eur   at 5 o'clock

tas father   **dha das** your father
mamm mother   **y vamm** his mother

The third mutation (column 3) occurs after **ow**, 'my', **hy**, 'her', **aga**, 'their' and the number three, **tri** and **teyr**:

tas father   **aga thas** their father
penn head   **ow fenn** my head
ki dog   **hy hi** her dog

The fourth mutation (column 4) comes after **ow** making a verb into a present participle. These are used with the long forms of **bos**, 'to be':

bos to be   **ow pos** being
dybri to eat   **ow tybri** eating
gwari to play   **ow kwari** playing

The fifth mutation (column 5) is found after **ple?**, 'where?' and **p'eur?**, 'when?'

Table of mutations

1	2 soft	3 breathed	4 hard	5 mixed
B	V		P	F
CH	J			
D	DH		T	T
G	- or W*		K	H
K	G	H		
M	V			F
P	B	F		
T	D	TH		

*gwedrenn > **an wedrenn**, the glass
*gorvarghas > **an worvarghas**, the supermarket

Plurals

In English most nouns add an 's' in the plural (e.g. 'house', 'houses').

In Cornish most nouns add –**ow**: **chi**, 'house', **chiow**, 'houses. However there are a lot of irregular ones and these are shown in the Glossary (pages 46-48).

Adjectives

Adjectives are describing words and in Cornish they normally come after the noun. Watch out for mutations after feminine singular nouns!
ki dog, **gwynn** white
ki gwynn a white dog
kador chair, **koth** old
kador goth an old chair
den man, **bras** big
den bras a big man
edhen bird, **du** black
edhen dhu a black bird

Verbs

Verbs in Cornish can also be nouns e.g.:
kana means 'to sing' or 'singing';
da yw genev kana, 'I like to sing' or 'I like singing'
gwari, 'to play' or 'playing';
gwell yw gensi gwari, 'she prefers to play' or 'she prefers playing'.

Verbs can be made by using the long form of **bos**, 'to be' as shown on page 42:

yth esov vy ow mos	I am going
yma hi ow tonsya	she is dancing
ymons i ow kwari	they are playing

You can also make verbs by putting the subject first. The subject is the person doing the action and can be any person or noun. This is followed by **a** which causes the second mutation (table on left) and then the stem of the verb, usually the verb with the last syllable taken off. Some examples:

neuvya to swim		**my a neuv** I swim	
seni to play (music)		**hi a sen** she plays	
redya to read		**Jori a red** George reads	
donsya to dance		**i a dhons** they dance	
gweles to see		**an ki a wel** the dog sees	
klywes to hear		**ev a glyw** he hears	
treylya to turn		**an karr a dreyl** the car turns	
lywya to drive		**ni a lyw** we drive	
prena to buy		**ty a bren** you buy	

'A', 'an' and 'the'

English 'a' and 'an' are called the indefinite article. These are not needed in Cornish so:

daras means 'door' or 'a door'
aval means 'apple' or 'an apple'

English 'the' is called the definite article and is **an** in Cornish. This causes a mutation of feminine nouns starting with the letters shown in the table at the top of this page.

an daras 'the door'
an aval 'the apple',
but …
an voes 'the table' (from feminine **moes**)
an gador 'the chair' (from feminine **kador**)
an bel 'the ball' (from feminine **pel**)

'Some', 'any'

These are not expressed in Cornish, so:

yma keus war an voes, there is (some) cheese on the table
eus leth y'n amari? Is there (any) milk in the cupboard?

Answers to puzzles

Page 5
How are you?

yn studh euthek
yn studh drog
da lowr
yn poynt da
pur dha

Page 7
What are they called?

Y hanow yw Peder
Hy hanow yw Maria
Aga henwyn yw Alan ha Yowann.
Ow hanow yw ...

Who is who?

Mighal is talking to Yowann.
Anna is talking to Lowena.
Mighal is the person in the green bathing cap.
Yowann is speaking to Mighal.
Jori is reading the paper.
Jori is going home.

Can you remember?

Pyth yw dha hanow?
Ow hanow yw ...
Hanow ow howethes yw Jenifer.
Ottomma ow howethes Jenifer.
Hanow ow howeth yw Gawen?

Page 9
Can you remember?

bleujenn, kath, gwydhenn, neyth, edhen, chi, howl, fenester, karr, ki.

Page 11
Who comes from where?

Hans come from Germany.
The Indians are called Hari and Indira.
Lolita is Spanish.
Yuri lives in Moscow.
Yes, Angus is the Scottish contestant.
Marie and Pierre come from France.
Moscow is in Russia.

Page 13
How old are they?

Mighal is nearly 14; Maria and Kerys are 15; Jori is 12; Morwenna is 11; Dewi is 9; Talwynn is 5.

Brothers and sisters

A = Maria and Kerys; B = Dewi
C = Mighal; D = Jori; E = Morwenna

Page 17
Where is everyone?

Yma mamm-wynn y'n esedhva.
Yma Simon y'n gegin.
Yma Isabella war-wartha.
Yma Peder y'n stevell-omwolghi.
Yma an tarosvann yn chambour Isabella.
Yma tas-gwynn y'n stevell-dhybri.

Can you remember?

Trigys ov vy y'n dre.
Trigys os ta y'n pow.
Trigys yw mamm-wynn yn rannji.
Trigys on ni yn chi.
Yma an stevell-omwolghi war-wartha.
Yma Simon y'n gibell.

Page 19
Where are the animals hiding?

Yma an hamster y'n seth bleujennow.
Yma an gath vyghan a-dryv an bellwolok.
Yma an ki byghan y'n amari.
Yma an boejji war an estyllenn.
Yma an sarf a-rag an gweli-dydh.
Yma an velhwyoges ryb an pellgowser.

Page 21
Who likes what

Pyran likes cheese.
Yowann doesn't like ham
Grandfather prefers grapes to bananas.

Page 23
Who is saying what?

'Yma nown dhymm!'
'Eus nown dhis?'
'Omserv!'
'Ystynn dhymm gwedrenn, mar pleg.'
'Eus hwans dhis a askloes?'
'Eus, mar pleg.'
'Nag eus, My re dhybris lowr.'
'An boes yw pur dha.'

Page 25
What are they doing?

A Yma ev ow kegi
B Yma ev ow neuvya
C Ymons i ow tonsya
D Yma hi ow seni krowd
E Yma ev ow lymna

Questions and answers

Pyth esos ta ow kul? Yth esov vy ow kegi.
Pyth esos ta ow kul? Yth esov vy ow neuvya.
Pyth esowgh hwi ow kul? Yth eson ni ow tonsya.
Pyth esos ta ow kul? Yth esov vy ow seni krowd.
Pyth esos ta ow kul? Yth esov vy ow lymna.

Page 27
Mark's day

1B, 2E, 3F, 4A, 5H, 6G, 7D, 8C.

What is the time?

A   Pymp wosa teyr yw.
B   Pymp wosa unnek yw.
C   Deg dhe naw yw.
D   Kwarter dhe beder yw.
E   Pymp warn ugens wosa teyr yw.
F   Hanter wosa seyth yw.
G   Teyr eur yw.
H   Peder eur yw.
I   Naw eur yw.
J   Hanter wosa unn yw.
K   Pymp wosa seyth yw.
L   Hanter wosa deg yw.
M   Hwegh eur yw.
N   Pymp warn ugens dhe beder yw.
O   Pymp dhe dhyw yw.

Page 29
Your diary for the week

Dy' Gwener, my a wra donsya gans Jori.
Dy' Meurth, my a wra neuvya.
Dy' Sadorn, my a wra gwari peldroes.

Page 33
In Trenowydh

Ple'ma an varghas, mar pleg?
Eus koffiji yn ogas?
Kemmer an tressa fordh a-dheghow ha ke war ewn.
Kemmer an tressa fordh a-gledh hag ena war ewn.
To the cafe.

Page 37
Buying fruit

Peswar lymmaval, kilo bananas ha pinaval, mar pleg.
Peswar lymmaval: 80 diner.
Bananas: £1.80 an kilo.
Pinaval: £1.60. Warbarath: £4.20
Avalow a gost £2.00 an kilo.
Unn pinaval a gost £1.60.
Brykedh a gost £1.80 an kilo.

Page 39
When are their birthdays?

Penn-bloedh Wella yw an 21ens a vis Metheven.
Penn-bloedh Tegenn yw an 18ves a vis Hedra.
Penn-bloedh Maria yw an 31ens a vis Est.
Penn-bloedh Alan yw an 3a a vis Meurth.
Penn-bloedh Dewi yw an 7ves a vis Gwynngala.

Page 40
What colour is it?

An howl yw melyn. An to yw rudhvelyn. An fordh yw loes. An ebrenn yw glas. An bleujennow yw gwynnrudh. An edhen yw du. An karr yw rudh. An gwydh yw glas. An chi yw gwynn.

Glossary

abbreviations used:

m.   masculine
f.   feminine (feminine nouns will mutate after **an** 'the' if they begin with the letters **b, d, g, gw, k, m, t.** (see table on page 43)
s.   singular
pl.   plural
adj.   adjective
vb.   verb

The small superscript numbers ^{2} ^{3} ^{4} ^{5} refer to the mutations caused:

kath; an^2 **g**ath
tas; ow^3 **th**as
dybri; ow^4 **t**ybri (see page 42)
Plurals are shown by **+ow, +yow, +s** e.g. **dowr** 'water' **+ow dowrow** 'waters'.

Irregular plurals are shown in full e.g. **hanow** 'name', **henwyn** 'names'.

---

a ble^5? *from where?*
a^2 vynn'ta? *do you want?*
a^2 *from*
a^2-dal *opposite*
a^2-dheghow *right, on the right*
a^2-dravydh *for nothing, don't mention it*
a-dryv *behind*
aga^3 *their*
agan *our*

agas *pl. your*
a^2-gledh *left, on the left*
Alban *Scotland*
Almayn *Germany*
amanenn *m.* **+ow** *butter*
amari *m.* **+ow** *cupboard*
an *the*
an gwella *the best*
arghans *m. money*
arghantti *m.* **+ow** *bank*
askloesenn *f.* **askloes** *chip*
aval *m.* **+ow** *apple*
aval-kerensa *m.*
avalow-kerensa *tomato*
a-vorow *tomorrow*
ayrborth *m.* **+ow** *airport*

banana +s *banana*
bara *m. bread*
bara byghan *m. roll, bun*
bleujenn *f.* **+ow** *flower*
blydhen *f.* **blydhynyow** *year*
boes *m. food*
boesti *m.* **+ow** *restaurant*
bras *adj. big, large*
broder *m.* **breder** *brother*
brykedhenn *f.* **brykedh** *apricot*
byghan *adj. small*
bys yn *until*

chi *m.* **+ow** *house*
choklet *m. chocolate*
chymbla *m.* **chymblow** *chimney*

da *adj. good*
da lowr *good enough, O.K.*
da yw genev ... *I like ...*
daffar ilow *m. musical instrument*
daras *m.* **+ow** *door*
deg *ten*
degves *tenth*
dell yw usyes *usually*
deus! *s. come!*

devedhys *come from*
dew^2 *m. two*
dewdhek *twelve*
dewgh! *pl. come!*
Dewi *David*
dew-ugens *forty*
dha *s. your*
dha weles! *s. see you! goodbye*
dhe^2 *to*
dhis *s. to you*
diw^2 *f. two*
dohajydh *m.* **+yow** *afternoon*
dohajydhweyth *in the afternoon*
dons *m.* **+yow** *dance*
donsya *vb. to dance*
dos *vb. to come*
dowr *m.* **+ow** *water*
drog *adj. bad*
du *adj. black*
dy' Gwener *Friday*
dy' Lun *Monday*
dy' Mergher *Wednesday*
dy' Meurth *Tuesday*
dy' Sadorn *Saturday*
dy' Sul *Sunday*
dy' Yow *Thursday*
dybri *vb. to eat* **ow tybri** *eating*
dydh *m. day* **+yow (an jydh** *the day)*
dydh da! *good day!*
dyenn rew *m.* **dyennow rew** *ice-cream*
Dyw *m.* **+ow** *God*
dyw genes! *goodbye!*
edhen *f.* **ydhyn** *bird*
eglos *f.* **+yow** *church*
ena *then, there*
estyllenn *f.* **estyll** *shelf*
etek *eighteen*
eth *eight*
ethves *eighth*
eus? *is/are there?*
euthek *adj. awful*
ewnter *m.* **ewntres** *uncle*
eyl *second*
Eynda *India*

fatell? *how?*
fatla genes? *s. how are you?*
fenester *f.* **fenestri** *window*
froeth *pl. fruit*
Frynkek *adj. French*

gav dhymm *excuse me*
gell *adj. brown*
glas *blue, green*
gols *m. hair*
gorsav *m.* **+ow** *station*
gorsav petrol *petrol station*
gorthugher *m. evening*
gorthugherweyth *in the evening*
gorvarghas *f.* **+ow** *supermarket*
goslowes orth *vb. to listen to*
gul *vb. to do*
gwari *vb. to play (a game)* **ow kwari** *playing*
gwav *m.* **+ow** *winter*
gwedrenn *f.* **+ow** *glass*
gwedrennas *m.* **+ow** *glassful*
gweli *m.* **+yow** *bed*
gweli-dydh *m.* **gweliow-dydh** *sofa*
gwell *adj. better*
gwell yw genev ... *I prefer ...*
gwenton *m. spring (season)*
gwerthji *m.* **+ow** *shop*
gwesti *m.* **+ow** *guest house*
gwia *vb. to weave, knit*
gwinreunenn *f.*
gwinreun *grape*
gwrav *I do*
gwruthyl traow *vb. to create things*
gwydhenn *f.* **gwydh, tree*

gwynn *adj. white*
gwynnrudh *adj. pink*
gwyrdh *adj. green*

ha *and (***hag** *before a vowel)*
hamburger *m. +s hamburger*
hamster *m. +s hamster*
haneth *tonight*
hanow *m.* **henwyn** *name*
hansel *m. +yow breakfast*
hanterdydh *m. midday noon*
hanternos *f. midnight*
hav *m. +ow summer*
hedhyw *today*
hegar *adj. affectionate*
hel an dre *f.* **helyow an dre** *town hall*
hemma *m. this*
henna *m. that*
hir *adj. tall, long*
hobi *m. hobby*
hogenn froeth *f.*
hogennow-froeth *fruit tart*
hou! *hi! hello!*
howl *m. sun*
huni *one*
hwans *m. +ow wish*
hwegh *six*
hweghves *sixth*
hwetek *sixteen*
hwiles *vb. to look for*
hwoer *f.* **hwerydh** *sister*
hy[3] *her*

ilow *f. music*
Iwerdhon *Ireland*

Jori *George*
kador *f. +yow chair*

kampva *f. +ow camping site*
kans *m. +ow hundred*
karr *m.* **kerri** *car*
karrji *m. +ow garage*
kartenn bost *f.*
**kartennow post postcard*
kath *f. +es cat*
kavoes *vb. to find, get*
ke *m. +ow hedge*
kegi *vb. to cook*
Kembra *Wales*
Kembrek *adj. Welsh*
kemmeres *vb. to take*
kerens *pl. parents*
Kernewek *adj. Cornish*
Kernow *Cornwall*
keus *m. +yow cheese*
kevywi *m. +ow party*
kewsel *vb. to speak*
ki *m.* **keun** *dog*
kig *m. +yow meat*
kikti *m. +ow butcher's shop*
kilo *m. +s kilo*
kinyow *m.* **kinyewow dinner*
klavji *m. +ow hospital*
koffi *m. coffee*
koffiji *m. +ow coffee house*
kola *m. cola*
koth *adj. old*
koweth *m. +a friend*
kowethes *f. +ow friend*
kroglenn *f. +ow curtain*
krowd *m. +ys violin*
kwarter *m.* **kwartrys quarter*
kymyst *m. +yon chemist*
kynsa *first*
kynyav *m. +ow autumn*
kyst *f. +yow box*

kyst-lyther *f.*
kystyow-lyther *letter-box*
lavar dhymm *tell me*
leth *m. milk*
letusenn *f.* **letus lettuce*
leurlenn *f. +ow carpet*
leverel *vb. to say, tell*
liv *f. +yow lunch*
liter *m.* **litrow** *litre*
loes *adj. grey*
log bellgowser *f.*
**logow pellgowser phone box*
losow-kegin *pl. vegetables*
lowr *adj. enough*
lymmaval *m. +ow lemon* **lemonade**
lymna *vb. to paint*
lyver *m.* **lyvrow** *book*
lywya *vb. to drive*

mamm *f. +ow mother*
mamm-wynn *f.*
**mammow-gwynn grandmother*
mar pleg *please*
marghas *f. +ow market*
Maria *Mary*
melhwyoges *f. tortoise*
melyn *adj. yellow, blonde*
mes *but*
meur ras *thanks*
Mighal *Michael*
mil *m. +yow thousand*
mires orth *vb. to watch, look at*
mis *m. +yow month*
mis-Du *m. November*
mis-Ebryl *m. April*
mis-Est *m. August*
mis-Genver *m. January*
mis-Gortheren *m. July*

mis-Gwynngala *m. September*
mis-Hedra *m. October*
mis-Hwevrer *m. February*
mis-Kevardhu *m. December*
mis-Me *m. May*
mis-Metheven *m. June*
mis-Meurth *m. March*
modrep *f.* **modrebedh aunt*
moes *f. +ow table*
mordhos hogh *f. ham*
mos *vb. to go*
my a garsa *I would like + verb*
mynysenn *f.* **mynys minute*
myttin *m. +yow morning*
myttinweyth *m. in the morning*

na ... na *neither...nor*
naw *nine*
nawves *ninth*
nebes *m. some, a bit*
neppyth *something*
neppyth arall? *anything else?*
nessa *adj. next*
neuvya *vb. to swim*
neyth *m. +ow nest*
nos *f. +ow night*
nown *m. hunger*
nownsek *nineteen*
ny allav *I can't*
ny[2] *not*
nyns eus dhymm *I don't have*
nyns yw da genev *I don't like*

ogas *adj. near*
ogas ha *nearly*
oll *adj. all*

omservya *vb. to serve oneself*
onan *one*
ostel *f.* **+yow** *hotel*
ostel yowynkneth *f. youth hostel*
ottomma *here is*
ow³ *my*
ow⁴ *-ing*
owraval *m.* **+ow** *orange (fruit)*
oy *m.* **+ow** *egg*

Peder *Peter*
peder *f. four*
peldroes *f. football*
pell *adj. far*
pellgowser *m. telephone*
pellwolok *f. television*
penn-bloedh *m.*
pennow-bloedh *birthday*
pes bloedh? *how many years? how old?*
pes? *how many?*
peswar *m. four*
peswara *fourth*
peswardhek *fourteen*
peswar-ugens *eighty*
p'eur⁵? *when?*
piano *m.* **+s** *piano*
pinaval *m.* **+ow** *pineapple*
pitsa *m.* **+s** *pizza*
piw? *who?*
ple'ma? *where is?*
ple⁵? *where?*
po *or*
poeth *adj. hot*
poll neuvya *m.* **pollow neuvya** *swimming pool*
popti *m.* **+ow** *bakery*
Pow Frynk *France*
Pow Sows *England*
prena *vb. to buy*
prenassa *vb. to go shopping*
privedhyow *pl. toilets*

prys-boes *m.*
prysyow-boes *mealtime*
pub *adj. each, every*
pub huni *each one*
pur dha *very good*
pur² *very*
py eur yw? *what is the time?*
py kost yw? *how much is it?*
pymp *five*
pympes *fifth*
pymthek *fifteen*
pysk *m.* **puskes** *fish*
pyth? *what?*

redya *vb. to read*
reken *m.* **reknow** *bill*
ris *m. rice*
rosenn *f.* **+ow** *rose*
rudh *adj. red*
rudhvelyn *adj. orange (colour)*
Russi *Russia*
ryb *by, next to*

sarf *f.* **serf** *snake*
selsigenn *f.* **selsik** *sausages*
seni *vb. to play (an instrument)*
seth *m.* **+ow** *vase*
sevel *vb. to rise, get up*
seytek *seventeen*
seyth *seven*
seythves *seventh*
skol *f.* **+yow** *school*
soedhva *f.* **+ow** *office*
Soedhva an Post *The Post Office*
soedhva dherivadow *f. information office*
soper *m. supper*
Sowsnek *adj. English*
spagetti *m. spaghetti*
Spayn *Spain*
Spaynek *adj. Spanish*

spisti *m.* **+ow** *grocer's shop*
sport *m.* **+ow** *sport*
stret *m.* **+ow** *street*
studh *m.* **+yow** *state, condition*
sugen *m.* **+yow** *juice*
sugen froeth *m. fruit juice*

tamm *m.* **temmyn** *bit*
tamm vydh *not at all*
tanow *adj. thin*
tas *m.* **+ow** *father*
tas-gwynn *m.* **tasow-wynn** *grandfather*
te *m. tea*
tennis *m. tennis*
tesenn *f.* **+ow** *cake*
tew *adj. fat*
teylu *m.* **+yow** *family*
teyr³ *f. three*
to *m.* **+how** *roof*
tressa *third*
treylya *vb. to turn*
tri³ *m. three*
triga *vb. to live*
trigys *adj. resident*
tri-ugens *sixty*
troes *m.* **treys** *foot*
trydhek *thirteen*

ugens *twenty*
ugensves *twentieth*
unn *adj. one*
unnek *eleven*

war droes *on foot*
war ewn *straight on*
war tu ha *towards, about (time)*
warbarth *(all)together*
wosa *after, past*

y² *his*
yma dhymm ... *I have (own)...*
yn *in*
y'n *in the*

yn-hons *over there*
yn mysk *among*
yn ogas *nearby*
yn poynt da *in good health*
yn-dann *under*
ynwedh *also*
Yowann *John*
yowynk *adj. young*
ystynna *vb. to pass*
ytho *so, then*
yw da genes? *do you like?*

For further information on Cornish, contact **Kesva an Taves Kernewek** (The Cornish Language Board):

☎ and fax 01736850878
e.mail
jansell@kesva.co.uk

☎01579382511
e.mail
mpierce@kesva.co.uk

First published in Cornish 2006 by **Kesva an Taves Kernewek** (The Cornish Language Board), copyright © Kesva an Taves Kernewek. Copyright 2001, 1986 Usborne Publishing Linited, London